7 Life Gems of Total Happiness: For Pets

Ashely Williams, Curtis Williams
&
Eureka Williams

© Copyright 2025, Ashely Williams, Curtis Williams & Eureka Williams

All Rights Reserved

No part of this book may be reproduced, stored in a retrieval system, or transmitted, in any form or by any means, electronic, mechanical, photocopying, recording, or otherwise, without prior written permission from the publisher, except for brief quotations embodied in critical reviews and certain other noncommercial uses permitted by copyright law.

ISBN:

978-1-0881-0499-6

Introduction

In this introduction, we delve into the profound concept of happiness as a dynamic and vibrant spectrum, much like the hues of a rainbow, with each color representing a distinct and essential aspect of our lives. Just as the individual colors of the rainbow blend harmoniously to create its breathtaking beauty, every facet of our well-being works in unison to form the complete and intricate picture of happiness.

Our pets, those unwavering and devoted companions, influence nearly every corner of our existence. Through their unconditional love, loyalty, and companionship, they provide a unique form of support that nourishes and enriches multiple dimensions of our lives, including our spiritual, intellectual, emotional, financial, environmental, physical, and social well-being.

By examining happiness through the framework of the 7 Rainbow Gems of Happiness, we will explore how pets contribute far beyond mere companionship, offering a deep sense of joy, balance, and fulfillment. Their presence in our lives acts as a guide, helping us navigate the complex layers of existence and prompting personal growth along the way. They are not only animals that we care for, but they are also partners in our journey toward greater self-awareness, joy, and resilience. Together, we will uncover how these beloved animals enhance our lives, helping us become more connected with ourselves and the world around us.

Table of Contents

Chapter 1 1

Red – Spiritual Happiness: The Heartfelt Connection 1

Chapter 2 6

Orange – Pet Intellectual Happiness 6

Chapter 3 12

Yellow – Emotional Happiness 12

Chapter 4 17

Green – Financial Happiness: Managing Resources with Pets 17

Chapter 5 23

Blue – Environmental Happiness: Creating Harmony around Us 23

Chapter 6 29

Indigo – Physical Happiness: The Vitality of Life 29

Chapter 7 34

Violet – Social Happiness: Building Connections 34

Conclusion: The Rainbow of Happiness 39

Chapter 1

Red – Spiritual Happiness: The Heartfelt Connection

The color red is a symbol of passion, energy, and strength. It represents the foundational forces that anchor us, providing a sense of security and stability in a world that can often feel uncertain and chaotic. Just as red brings to mind vitality and grounding, pets serve as powerful anchors in our lives, offering comfort, stability, and a deep sense of safety. Their unwavering love creates a profound spiritual connection, helping us feel more grounded, present, and aligned with both ourselves and the world around us. In this chapter, we will explore how pets nurture our spiritual happiness, guiding us toward a deeper sense of inner peace and a more mindful, fulfilling existence.

One of the most profound aspects of having a pet is the sacred bond that forms between them and their owner. This bond is rooted in unconditional love—a love that is pure, consistent, and free from judgment. Unlike many human relationships, pets love us without expectation or condition. Whether we are experiencing joy or facing challenges, our pets remain by our side, offering their affection and companionship without asking for anything in return. This type of love serves as a powerful lesson in the nature of unconditional love: it does not need to be earned or proven. Pets do not require us to be perfect. They simply love us for who we are, and in doing so, they remind us to love others in the same way—without conditions, expectations, or judgments. Their loyalty and affection help us embrace the beauty of loving freely and without reservation.

As we deepen the bond with our pets, we experience growth in compassion and kindness. Caring for a pet opens our hearts to a more selfless, unconditional form of love. This connection allows us to move beyond surface-level interactions and tap into a deeper well of empathy. Pets also teach us the importance of living in the present moment. While humans often dwell on past regrets or future worries, pets live fully in the here and now. They savor each moment—whether it's a walk in the park, a cozy nap, or a playful game. By observing and being with our pets, we learn to slow down, embrace the beauty of each moment, and practice mindfulness. Their ability to stay present reminds us to let go of distractions and engage fully in our lives.

This mindfulness goes beyond just being aware of the present; it extends into how we care for others. Pets teach us to offer our love freely, without expectation, and to appreciate life as it unfolds—imperfections and all. Their unconditional affection helps us cherish the small moments that might otherwise go unnoticed. Whether it's the warmth of their companionship or the joy of seeing them excited, pets remind us of the beauty in simplicity. Their presence encourages us to appreciate the ordinary moments and to extend love to others with authenticity and kindness.

Through the spiritual bond we share with our pets, we are guided toward personal growth and self-discovery. This connection fosters a sense of peace, joy, and fulfillment that is not reliant on external circumstances. The love we receive from our pets nurtures our hearts, encouraging us to live with greater awareness, intention, and presence. By caring for them, we deepen our connection to the world around us, cultivating a sense of unity and belonging. The spiritual lessons our pets teach us help us to better understand ourselves and the world, leading to a more harmonious and peaceful existence.

In conclusion, pets play an essential role in our journey toward spiritual happiness. Their love heals us, their presence invites us to embrace the present moment, and the bond we share with them strengthens our connection to the world. As we spend time with our pets, we learn to practice unconditional love, grow spiritually, and reconnect with our true selves. Through their simple yet profound presence, pets lead us toward a deeper understanding of love, peace, and joy. In doing so, they guide us to a happiness that transcends the ordinary, bringing us closer to the heart of what it truly means to live a fulfilling and meaningful life.

Chapter 2

Orange – Pet Intellectual Happiness

Orange is the color of creativity, curiosity, and intellectual engagement. It symbolizes the vibrant energy that sparks new ideas and encourages us to think critically and outside the box. In this chapter, we will explore how pets play an essential role in fostering intellectual happiness, stimulating our minds, and nurturing our curiosity. Whether through problem-solving, training, or simply learning how to care for them, pets encourage us to engage our brains in ways that promote continuous intellectual growth.

Pets as Intellectual Teachers

Pets are more than just adorable companions—they are also excellent teachers. They inspire us to think creatively and challenge us to problem-solve. Training a dog to learn a new trick, for instance, requires us to think strategically and use our creativity to figure out the most effective way to communicate with them. The process involves understanding their needs, behaviors, and learning styles, which encourages us to think critically about how to approach each situation. Similarly, managing behavioral issues, such as teaching a cat not to knock things off the table or preventing a dog from jumping on guests, requires problem-solving skills that stretch our mental capacities.

Pets also encourage us to be curious about the world around us, much like they are constantly exploring their environment. Whether it's a dog sniffing a new scent or a cat investigating a hidden corner, pets are always discovering new things. By observing their natural curiosity, we are reminded to stay inquisitive and explore the world with the same enthusiasm. Watching pets figure out problems, such as how to open a door or find a hidden treat, inspires us to think more creatively and engage our own problem-solving abilities.

Learning from Our Pets

Spending time with pets can teach us a great deal about the world of animals and even about ourselves. While pets cannot communicate with words, their actions and behaviors are a form of communication that can offer us valuable insights. For example, a dog might sense when we are upset or anxious, and a cat might find an unconventional hiding spot when they need space. By observing these behaviors, we gain a better understanding of animal instincts and emotional intelligence.

In addition, pets teach us patience and persistence. Training a pet, whether it's a dog learning a new command or a cat getting used to a new environment, requires time, patience, and dedication. The process of teaching them encourages us to develop these qualities in ourselves. We learn that intellectual growth is not instantaneous but a gradual process that involves trial, error, and ongoing effort. This lesson is particularly powerful in a world that often demands quick results, as it reminds us of the value of patience and steady progress.

Pets also serve as a reminder that learning is a lifelong journey. As we engage with our pets, we are continually learning new things—not just about them but also about ourselves and how we approach challenges. Their ability to adapt, learn, and grow in response to their environment is a constant source of inspiration, pushing us to stay open to new experiences and deepen our understanding of the world.

Mental Stimulations and Play

Engaging in activities with pets is not only fun, but it also provides mental stimulation for both us and them. Training pets, solving puzzles, and playing games all require focus, strategy, and creativity. For example, when teaching a dog to fetch a specific toy or encouraging a pet to solve a puzzle, both the pet and the owner are mentally engaged. The pet has to understand the task, and the owner must devise a strategy to teach and guide them. This shared mental challenge promotes intellectual growth for both parties.

Agility courses, training sessions, and interactive play are excellent ways to keep both pets and humans mentally active. These activities encourage creativity, patience, and problem-solving. Teaching new tricks or engaging in complex games requires us to think on our feet, and pets benefit by developing new skills, improving their mental acuity, and strengthening their bond with us.

Interactive mental games, such as puzzle toys, treat challenges, or hide-and-seek, provide opportunities for both the pet and owner to exercise their brains. These games promote intellectual growth by encouraging pets to think critically about how to access rewards, and by involving the owner in the process, they help develop problem-solving strategies that improve the relationship between pet and humans. Through these playful, stimulating activities, both pets and owners continue to learn and grow intellectually.

Conclusion

Pets are an incredible catalyst for intellectual happiness. They inspire us to think creatively, challenge us to solve problems, and encourage us to stay curious and open-minded. Whether through training, solving puzzles, or observing their unique ways of interacting with the world, pets foster an environment of continuous learning and mental stimulation. The intellectual engagement they offer helps keep our minds sharp and encourages us to approach challenges with creativity and patience. In return, we help our pets grow and thrive, making the intellectual bond we share a rewarding and mutually beneficial journey of discovery and growth.

Chapter 3

Yellow – Emotional Happiness

Yellow, the color of sunshine and warmth, symbolizes emotional well-being, joy, and balance. It invokes feelings of comfort, positivity, and emotional stability, guiding us toward greater happiness. In this chapter, we explore how pets help us cultivate emotional happiness by providing unwavering support in times of stress, anxiety, and loneliness. Their presence creates an emotional sanctuary where we can heal and grow, both in times of difficulty and in our everyday lives.

The Emotional Healing of Pets

Pets have an incredible ability to heal our emotional wounds. When we face sadness, stress, or hardship, the simple act of interacting with a pet can be a powerful form of emotional therapy. Whether it's the soft fur of a dog under your hand, the soothing purr of a cat in your lap, or the gentle sounds of a bird's chirping, pets have an innate ability to bring comfort when we need it most.

In our lowest moments, pets offer unconditional love without asking for anything in return. They don't judge, they don't question, and they don't require explanations. Their presence alone is enough to calm anxious thoughts and ease troubled hearts. The quiet companionship of a pet can help reduce anxiety, relieve stress, and bring us back to a place of emotional peace. The comforting nudge of a dog or the warmth of a cat nestled beside us provides a safe space, where we can rest, heal, and reclaim our emotional well-being.

Pets as Emotional Anchors

One of the greatest gifts pets offers is the stability they provide in our lives. In a world that can often feel chaotic or uncertain, the unconditional love and loyalty of a pet remain constant. They are always there for us, waiting eagerly to greet us, no matter the ups and downs of our day. This stability makes pets emotional anchors, offering comfort and support in ways that few other relationships can.

After a challenging day at work, school, or in our personal lives, the knowledge that a pet is waiting for us at home brings a sense of grounding. The consistent presence of a pet creates a deep sense of emotional security, offering reassurance that we are not alone. Whether it's a dog's joyful tail wagging or a cat curling up contentedly by our side, pets are a reminder that there is always something stable and unwavering in our lives, no matter how unpredictable the world may feel.

Pets are not just companions; they are emotional supporters. They remind us of our worth, provide comfort, and offer a sense of belonging. In this way, pets act as anchors that help us stay emotionally centered, even when everything around us feels uncertain. They teach us the value of loyalty and the importance of giving and receiving love without condition.

Boosting Our Mood

Pets have a remarkable ability to lift our spirits and brighten our lives. Their playful antics, affectionate nature, and genuine presence bring joy into our daily routines. Whether it's watching a dog excitedly chase after a ball or seeing a cat playfully bat at a toy, these moments of fun inject lightheartedness and laughter into our days.

But the joy that pets bring is not confined to their playful moments alone. They help us slow down and appreciate the small things in life. A dog's eager greeting or a cat curling up on our lap is a simple, yet profound reminder of how wonderful it is to be loved and cared for. These small moments help us reconnect with the present, finding joy in the here and now. Through their companionship, pets teach us how to be present, how to embrace the moment, and how to appreciate the little things that bring happiness.

Spending time with our pets instantly boosts our mood. Their presence calms our anxieties, lifts our spirits, and helps us feel more emotionally balanced. The affection and companionship they provide creates a sense of emotional stability and positivity. By simply being with our pets, we experience a sense of joy and emotional resilience that helps us face life with a more optimistic outlook.

Conclusion

Pets offer us a form of emotional support that is both profound and transformative. Their unconditional love, loyalty, and playful nature help us manage stress, anxiety, and loneliness. Whether it's the comfort of their presence, the joy of their playful antics, or the deep emotional bond we share with them, pets create a safe emotional space for healing and growth.

Through their warmth, affection, and loyalty, pets foster happiness, stability, and emotional security. They help us experience emotional fulfillment and teach us what it means to truly be happy.

The unconditional love and companionship they offer enable us to grow emotionally, experience true joy, and feel a sense of emotional balance that is grounded in the simple, yet powerful bond we share with them. Through their presence, pets help us discover a deeper understanding of emotional well-being and a more meaningful, fulfilled life.

Chapter 4

Green – Financial Happiness: Managing Resources with Pets

Green, the color of growth, abundance, and prosperity, symbolizes a flourishing and balanced life, representing harmony and well-being. In this chapter, we'll explore the practical aspects of pet ownership, including the financial responsibilities involved and the unexpected ways pets can help us manage our resources. While caring for a pet does come with a financial commitment, it also offers valuable lessons in budgeting, frugality, and making smart financial decisions that can benefit our lives in the long run.

The Costs of Pet Ownership

Owning a pet is a significant financial responsibility. From food to healthcare, pets require regular attention and care, and this comes at a cost. While it's important to plan for the expenses that come with pet ownership, it's also possible to manage these costs effectively with a bit of foresight.

To start, there are regular expenses, such as purchasing food, grooming, and keeping up with routine vet visits. Pets also require occasional special treatments, vaccines, and sometimes, unexpected medical costs. Emergencies, like a sudden illness or injury, can be financially overwhelming if not anticipated. Setting aside a portion of your income each month for pet-related expenses ensures you're prepared for both routine care and unforeseen circumstances. This proactive approach to budgeting will help you maintain financial stability while providing the best care for your pet.

Pet insurance can be an excellent option for covering more significant medical expenses, though it's important to research policies and select one that fits your needs. Managing pet-related costs involves balancing your financial priorities, but with careful planning and regular saving, the financial burden can be much less stressful.

Saving Through Pet Care

While it may seem like owning a pet is an added expense, pets can help us save money in unexpected ways. For instance, owning a dog often means more outdoor activity, like walking, running, or hiking. These activities not only keep your dog healthy but also improve your own physical health. The more active you are, the fewer medical bills you may have over time, as regular exercise can reduce the risk of chronic conditions and lower healthcare costs in the long run.

Additionally, having a pet encourages healthier living habits. Rather than spending money on dining out or indulging in expensive entertainment, you might find yourself enjoying more cost-effective activities, such as cooking at home or engaging in outdoor adventures with your pet. These small lifestyle changes can add up to substantial savings over time, improving your overall financial well-being while also strengthening your bond with your pet.

Moreover, pets can be a reminder to focus on what's important—your health, your home, and your family. By taking care of your pet and choosing activities that benefit both your physical and financial well-being, you naturally embrace a more frugal lifestyle.

Financial Responsibility and Pets

One of the most valuable lessons pets teach us is financial responsibility. When you adopt a pet, you commit to their well-being, which requires careful financial planning. From budgeting for food and healthcare to setting aside funds for emergencies, having a pet teaches you to think long-term and manage your finances more effectively.

Pets help us prioritize. Instead of spending impulsively on items we don't need, we learn to focus on the essential providing for our pets. This mindset shift can extend to other areas of our lives, encouraging us to budget wisely and make thoughtful decisions about how we allocate our financial resources.

Taking care of a pet requires planning and foresight, and these skills are transferable to other aspects of life. Whether it's saving for future goals, planning for retirement, or managing monthly expenses, the financial lessons we learn from pet ownership can serve us well in the broader context of personal finance.

Conclusion

While the financial commitment of owning a pet is undeniable, pets also offer a unique opportunity to learn valuable lessons about managing resources. They teach us how to budget, prioritize, and make smarter financial decisions.

Beyond the costs of food, healthcare, and unexpected expenses, pets can encourage us to live healthier, more frugal lives, leading to long-term savings and financial stability.

In caring for our pets, we become better at managing our finances, learning responsibility, and making thoughtful decisions. Pets bring joy and companionship into our lives while offering us the chance to grow in our understanding of how to manage money wisely. By embracing these lessons, we not only take better care of our pets but also set ourselves on a path toward greater financial well-being.

Chapter 5

Blue – Environmental Happiness: Creating Harmony around Us

Blue, the color of communication, peace, which symbolizes calm and harmony. It represents balance, trust, and a sense of tranquility. In this chapter, we explore how pets help us foster a peaceful environment, not just within our homes but also in our broader surroundings. From making our homes, more comfortable to encouraging outdoor activities, pets play a significant role in creating harmony and connection with the world around us.

A Harmonious Home for Your Pet

A harmonious home is one where both pets and their owners feel safe, comfortable, and loved. Creating such a space benefits everyone in the household, as it nurtures a sense of well-being and tranquility. When we design a living space that caters to our pets' needs, we enhance their security and happiness, which in turn helps create a more peaceful environment for us.

For pets, a cozy bed, a designated play area, and a secure space to retreat when they need rest all contribute to a sense of calm. Likewise, knowing that our pets have everything they need can ease our minds, allowing us to relax. Whether it's making sure your dog has a soft, quiet spot to sleep or ensuring your cat has places to explore and hide, a peaceful home fosters emotional stability for both pets and owners.

Additionally, a calm environment improves the relationship between pets and their owners. When pets feel safe and loved, they are generally more relaxed and well-behaved, which in turn creates less stress for everyone. This positive dynamic helps to build a more balanced and connected home, where emotional well-being can thrive.

Pets and Sustainability

Pets can also be valuable allies in our journey toward environmental sustainability. By making conscious choices in pet care, we can reduce waste and lessen our environmental impact. For example, opting for natural, organic pet food, choosing biodegradable waste bags, or selecting toys made from sustainable materials can contribute to a healthier planet.

Beyond these specific actions, being mindful about our pet-related purchases often leads to broader environmental consciousness. For instance, using fewer plastic items, recycling pet packaging, or choosing eco-friendly pet care products can reduce waste. Small changes—like buying products made from renewable resources or cutting back on unnecessary disposable items—can collectively lead to significant environmental benefits. Teaching children to care for pets in environmentally responsible ways can also help foster sustainable habits that extend to other areas of life.

By choosing sustainability in our pets' care, we create a ripple effect that positively impacts the environment, ensuring that we protect the world for future generations.

Connecting with Nature

One of the most significant ways pets help us foster environmental happiness is by encouraging us to spend more time outdoors. Whether it's walking your dog, playing fetch in the park, or simply sitting outside with your cat, pets inspire us to enjoy the natural world and get outside. This not only strengthens our bond with nature but also provides us with much-needed breaks from the demands of daily life.

Spending time outdoors with pets opens up opportunities to observe and appreciate the beauty of the natural world. The simple joy of a dog bounding through the grass or a cat watching birds from a windowsill reminds us of the importance of the environment and the need to protect it. As we walk our dogs on wooded paths or enjoy the fresh air with our pets, we deepen our connection to nature and understand better the importance of caring for the planet.

Pets also teach us about the interconnectedness of life. By spending time with animals and being active outdoors, we gain a greater appreciation for the environment and the ecosystems that sustain it. These experiences help foster a sense of environmental responsibility, encouraging us to preserve the spaces where we and our pets find joy and peace.

Conclusion

Pets play an essential role in helping us create a peaceful and harmonious environment. From providing a loving and comfortable home for our pets to encouraging eco-friendly practices and time spent outdoors, they have a unique ability to enhance both our immediate surroundings and the broader world. Through thoughtful pet care, we can reduce our environmental footprint, strengthen our connection to nature, and foster a more peaceful, balanced life.

With pets by our side, we are reminded to communicate peacefully, to take joy in the world around us, and to live in a way that benefits not only ourselves but also the planet. Whether it's by making sustainable choices, enjoying the outdoors, or simply creating a serene home, pets help us cultivate harmony in our lives and inspire us to protect the environment for all living creatures. Through them, we learn to live with a greater sense of balance and responsibility—creating a peaceful, sustainable world for ourselves, our pets, and future generations.

Chapter 6

Indigo – Physical Happiness: The Vitality of Life

Indigo, the color of intuition, perception, and physical well-being, is closely linked to our sense of awareness and vitality. In this chapter, we delve into how pets enhance our physical health. From motivating us to stay active to lowering stress and fostering mindful habits, pets play a vital role in improving our overall vitality and physical well-being.

Exercise and Activity

One of the greatest benefits of pet ownership is the encouragement to stay physically active. Pets, especially dogs, require regular exercise—whether it's a walk around the block, a run through the park, or a game of fetch. This provides an excellent opportunity for their owners to get moving as well. The simple act of walking with your dog helps you stay fit while also benefiting your pet's health.

Even with cats, the need to engage them in play encourages physical activity, though it may look a bit different. Tossing a toy or engaging in interactive games helps keep both the pet and the owner active. Regular exercise not only benefits your pet's fitness level but also enhances your own. It can improve cardiovascular health, maintain muscle tone, and keep joints limber. Moreover, being outside in nature, walking with your pet or simply sitting in the fresh air, boosts your energy levels and improves your mood.

Pets not only inspire us to stay active, but they also help us maintain a consistent exercise routine, promoting long-term physical health.

Pets and Health

The physical health benefits of having a pet extend beyond just exercise. Studies have shown that pets can have a positive impact on our health in a variety of ways. For instance, spending time with pets has been linked to lower blood pressure, reduced stress, and even improved cardiovascular health. The soothing presence of a pet can provide a sense of calm, lowering anxiety and promoting relaxation.

When we interact with pets—whether by petting a dog or simply cuddling with a cat—our bodies release oxytocin, the "feel-good" hormone, which helps to reduce stress and elevate mood. These comforting moments are scientifically shown to lower levels of cortisol, a hormone associated with stress. The result is a reduction in physical tension and improved emotional well-being.

Furthermore, the companionship of a pet can help lower the risk of depression, which in turn improves our physical health. The emotional support that pets provide can be a powerful tool in maintaining a healthy state of mind, which has a direct and positive effect on our overall physical health.

Intuitive Physical Care

In addition to the tangible health benefits pets provide, they also teach us how to become more in tune with our own bodies. Pets, especially dogs and cats, have an incredible intuition and can often sense when we need comfort or care. In return, we learn to listen to our own bodies and understand when we need rest, exercise, or proper nutrition.

Pets encourage us to adopt healthier habits by modeling behaviors like regular exercise, play, and mindful eating. For instance, when we see our dog excitedly bounding around for a walk or our cat eating a balanced meal, we are reminded to pay attention to our own physical needs. Caring for our pets' health can prompt us to make better choices for ourselves, like incorporating more physical activity into our day or eating more nourishing foods.

By observing our pets' habits, we also learn the importance of being present and mindful. Just as our pets live in the moment, we can cultivate mindfulness in our own lives—recognizing when we need to slow down, engage in physical activity, or take time to relax and recharge.

Conclusion

Pets offer numerous physical benefits that contribute to our vitality and overall well-being. They encourage us to stay active, reduce stress, and practice healthier habits—leading to better fitness and health.

Through our bond with them, we learn to be more attuned to our own physical needs, fostering a deeper sense of self-care and well-being. Whether through exercise, relaxation, or adopting mindful habits, pets play an essential role in helping us live a more energetic and fulfilling life, enhancing both our physical and emotional vitality.

Chapter 7

Violet – Social Happiness: Building Connections

Violet is the color of higher consciousness, spiritual awareness, and social relationships. In this chapter, we explore how pets play a crucial role in enriching our social lives. From fostering new friendships to strengthening existing relationships, pets enhance our connections with others, reduce feelings of loneliness, and increase our sense of belonging and community. They teach us the power of social bonds and help us cultivate more meaningful, empathetic relationships.

Pets as Social Bridges

Pets are natural social bridges, often bringing people together in ways that might not happen otherwise.

Whether you're walking your dog through the neighborhood or taking your cat to the vet, pets provide an instant conversation starter, making it easier to connect with strangers. Pets offer a shared interest that helps break the ice and create bonds between people.

In addition, pets provide ample opportunities for social interaction in our communities. Dog parks, pet-friendly events, and even online pet forums allow pet owners to connect, share experiences, and form friendships. These interactions foster a sense of community, where people come together, support each other, and enjoy the common joy of being pet owners. By owning a pet, we tap into a larger social network, often finding companionship and connection in unexpected places.

Strengthening Relationships

Pets don't just help us meet new people; they also play a significant role in deepening existing relationships. For families, having a pet creates a shared sense of responsibility and joy. Caring for a pet together, whether it's walking the dog, feeding the cat, or playing fetch, creates bonding moments that bring family members closer. This shared responsibility strengthens teamwork, trust, and emotional connections, creating a supportive and nurturing environment.

Pets also help strengthen friendships by providing common ground. For those who share a love of animals, having a pet can be a powerful way to bond. Conversations about pets, exchanging pet care tips, or simply enjoying each other's company while interacting with animals, create opportunities for meaningful social interactions. In this way, pets act as social catalysts, helping people form new connections and solidify existing ones.

Social Skills and Empathy

Interacting with pets also enhances our social skills and emotional intelligence. Through our daily interactions with animals, we learn to communicate non-verbally and become more attuned to the emotions of others. For instance, by observing our pet's behavior, we become more sensitive to their needs, learning how to respond with care and understanding. These skills are transferable to human relationships, teaching us patience, responsibility, and the ability to provide emotional support.

Pets also foster empathy, as they help us understand the world from another perspective. When we care for our pets, we learn to recognize their feelings, whether it's excitement for playtime or the comfort they seek after a long day. This awareness strengthens our ability to empathize with others, helping us respond thoughtfully to the emotions and needs of those around us.

The lessons in empathy and understanding we gain from our pets make us better equipped to navigate human relationships, improving both our personal and professional connections.

Furthermore, pets help ease social anxiety and boost our confidence in social settings. Whether we're at a party, a gathering, or simply meeting new people, pets can make us feel more at ease. Their presence encourages positive interactions and creates an environment where openness and connection can flourish. By being a part of these social exchanges, pets help us form lasting relationships with others.

Conclusion

Pets play an essential role in our social happiness. They bridge gaps between strangers, deepen our existing bonds, and teach us valuable lessons in communication and empathy. By encouraging us to interact with others, share experiences, and communicate more effectively, pets help us create a sense of community and belonging. Through our relationship with our pets, we also strengthen our relationships with the people around us. In the process, we learn to value connection, understanding, and the joy of meaningful social bonds, enriching our lives in ways that go beyond words.

Conclusion: The Rainbow of Happiness

In this final chapter, we reflect on how the seven Rainbow Gems come together to form a complete and balanced sense of happiness. Each gem represents a different facet of joy, and through our pets, we can cultivate and enhance all of them. From emotional support to physical vitality, from deepening our spiritual awareness to creating meaningful social connections, pets enrich every aspect of our lives. Their love and companionship help us unlock our fullest potential for happiness, making life brighter, fuller, and more connected.

Living the Rainbow

To live the rainbow with pets means embracing all seven gems to create a life of well-being and balance. Each gem holds a unique key to happiness, and together, they form a holistic approach to living a joyful life.

- **Red, the spiritual happiness gem**, teaches us to be present and mindful. Our pets help us connect to the here and now, encouraging us to focus on the moment and appreciate the simple pleasures in life.

- **Orange, the intellectual happiness gem**, fosters curiosity and creativity. Pets often push us to think outside the box, whether it's by discovering new ways to play, training new skills, or problem-solving their quirky behaviors.

- **Yellow, the emotional happiness gem**, reminds us of the importance of comfort, connection, and support. Our pets provide these in abundance, offering unconditional love that nourishes our emotional well-being.

- **Green, the financial happiness gem**, encourages wise decision-making and responsibility. Pets teach us about the value of commitment and balance, reminding us to make thoughtful choices in all areas of our lives, including finances.

- **Blue, the environmental happiness gem**, helps us create peaceful, eco-friendly spaces. Pets guide us in cultivating harmonious environments that are good for both us and the planet, fostering serenity and sustainability in our homes.

- **Indigo, the physical happiness gem**, motivates us to stay active and healthy. Whether through walks, play, or simply being more conscious of our well-being, pets encourage us to care for our bodies and live a vibrant life.

- **Violet, the social happiness gem**, opens the door to deeper social connections. Pets act as bridges, helping us form relationships, deepen friendships, and build a sense of community.

By incorporating all these gems, we create a life that balances joy, health, and well-being. Pets serve as mirrors to our lives, reflecting and enhancing these aspects of happiness, guiding us toward becoming the best versions of ourselves.

The Lifelong Journey

The journey of happiness with pets is not a fleeting experience. It is a lifelong adventure, rich with lessons and moments of growth. From the excitement of bringing a new pet into our home to the calm and peaceful companionship of an aging animal, pets teach us to appreciate the beauty of happiness at every stage of life. Their unconditional love reminds us that true happiness is not something we chase in the future, but something we experience in the present, in the moments we share with them.

Pets are there through all phases of life, offering comfort in times of joy and hardship alike. As we evolve and grow, our pets continue to teach us how to live with curiosity, gratitude, and love. They remind us that happiness is a journey, one that unfolds with each step we take, side by side with our loyal companions.

Conclusion

The Rainbow of Happiness shows us that pets are more than just companions; they are essential to our happiness and well-being. Each of the seven Rainbow Gems is brought to life through the bond we share with our pets, helping us cultivate a life of deep, lasting happiness. By living the rainbow—embracing the lessons our pets teach us and incorporating these gems into our daily lives—we create a fulfilling, balanced existence.

The journey with our pets is a constant reminder that happiness is not a destination, but a way of being. With our pets by our side, we experience a richness of connection, joy, and growth that extends far beyond the ordinary. Together, we can live a life full of love, understanding, and the brightest hues of happiness.

Appendices

Appendix A

Practical Tips for Enhancing Happiness with Your Pet

- **Create a Comfortable Space**

Provide a designated, quiet, and safe area for your pet where they can rest and relax. Keep it clean and stocked with their favorite toys, bed, and essentials.

- **Exercise Together**

Make physical activity a daily habit. Walk, run, or play with your pet regularly to keep both of you healthy and active. Try new activities to keep things interesting.

- **Practice Mindful Interaction**

Spend quality time with your pet, being fully present and engaged. Pay attention to their cues and body language to ensure they feel loved and respected.

- **Provide Mental Stimulation**

Challenge your pet's mind with puzzles, new tricks, and interactive toys. Regular training sessions not only improve behavior but also strengthen your bond.

- **Foster Social Connections**

Take your pet to social settings like parks or pet-friendly events to meet other pets and owners. Introduce them to new environments to boost their social confidence.

- **Prioritize Health and Well-being**

Keep up with regular vet check-ups, vaccinations, grooming, and a balanced diet to ensure your pet remains healthy and comfortable.

- **Focus on Emotional Connection**

Be mindful of your emotional state, as pets are sensitive to their owners feelings. Use positive reinforcement, patience, and consistency to strengthen your emotional bond.

By incorporating these seven simple steps into your life with your pet, you'll foster their happiness and well-being while deepening your connection and creating a more fulfilling, balanced life together.

Appendix B

Seven Pet Care and Well-being Resources

1. **American Veterinary Medical Association (AVMA)**

The AVMA is a trusted source for veterinary care, pet health, and professional advice. It offers a wealth of information on preventive care, vaccinations, and general wellness tips for pets.

Website: www.avma.org

2. **Petfinder**

Petfinder is a platform for pet adoption that also provides valuable resources on responsible pet ownership. Learn about choosing the right pet, pet care essentials, and training tips.

Website: www.petfinder.com

3. **ASPCA (American Society for the Prevention of Cruelty to Animals)**

The ASPCA offers resources on pet adoption, rescue services, behavioral guidance, and cruelty prevention. It also provides useful advice on pet health, emergency preparedness, and safety.

Website: www.aspca.org

4. The Humane Society of the United States

A leading advocate for animal welfare, the Humane Society offers resources on pet care, adoption, and animal protection. It provides educational materials on pet behavior, training, and the importance of responsible pet ownership.

Website: www.humanesociety.org

5. PetMD

PetMD is a comprehensive online resource for pet health. It provides expert articles on pet care, including topics on nutrition, grooming, medical issues, and emergency care.

Website: www.petmd.com

6. The Association of Professional Dog Trainers (APDT)

APDT is a valuable resource for dog owners looking for training advice and behavior solutions. The site offers expert tips, training techniques, and a directory to find certified trainers.

Website: www.apdt.com

7. The Good Dog Guide

This online guide helps pet owners find trusted pet care services, including groomers, trainers, and boarding facilities. It also offers advice on pet behavior and health care.

Website: www.thegooddogguide.com

Appendix C

Reflection Exercises to Deepen the Bond with Your Pet

1. Mindful Pet Observation

Set aside time each day to simply observe your pet. Watch their body language, their movements, and how they interact with their environment. Take note of what makes them happy, curious, or relaxed. Reflect on how your pet's behavior mirrors your own emotions or needs, and how this can deepen your connection.

2. Gratitude Journaling

Keep a journal where you write down moments of gratitude for your pet. Reflect on the joy, comfort, and lessons they bring into your life. Whether it's the companionship they offer or the unconditional love they provide, journaling can help you appreciate the positive impact your pet has on your happiness.

3. Shared Mindful Breathing

Sit quietly with your pet, focusing on your breath. Inhale deeply and slowly and encourage your pet to relax beside you. Sync your breathing with theirs if possible, creating a peaceful moment of connection. Reflect on the sense of calm this exercise brings, both for you and your pet, and how it strengthens your emotional bond.

4. Pet Appreciation Walk

Take your pet on a walk where the goal is simply to enjoy the surroundings and each other's company. Rather than rushing or focusing on exercise, spend time reflecting on your pet's companionship. Appreciate their presence and how they enhance your life. This mindful walk helps you bond through shared experience and appreciation.

5. Empathy Reflection

Take a moment to reflect on your pet's needs and feelings. Consider their daily routine and how they respond to various situations. Ask yourself how you can better understand and meet their emotional and physical needs. This exercise fosters a deeper sense of empathy, which strengthens your relationship with your pet.

6. Shared Playtime Reflection

Engage in a favorite activity with your pet—whether it's fetch, tug-of-war, or simply playing with toys. Afterward, reflect on how your pet responds to your energy and involvement. How does playtime affect your bond? Consider how play helps you both experience joy and connection in a meaningful way.

7. Silent Connection Time

Pet aside a quiet time to sit or lie down with your pet, without distractions. Whether it's simply cuddling or sitting in each other's presence, focus on the silent communication between you. Reflect on the unspoken connection you share. How does this peaceful moment enhance the bond between you and your pet, fostering a deeper sense of mutual understanding?

www.ingramcontent.com/pod-product-compliance
Lightning Source LLC
Chambersburg PA
CBHW050344010526
44119CB00049B/694